To Harriet, Duncan,
and all little explorers C.M.

For Anne, the loveliest,
the scrummiest, the best C.S.

Text copyright © 2000 Catherine Maccabe
Illustrations copyright © 2000 Clive Scruton
This edition copyright © 2000 Lion Publishing

The moral rights of the author and illustrator
have been asserted

First Augsburg Books edition. Originally published as *Teddy Bear, Piglet, Kitten & Me*
copyright © 2000 Lion Publishing plc., Sandy Lane West, Oxford, England.

Library of Congress Cataloging-in-Publication Data
ISBN 0-8066-4148-7
AF 9-4148

First edition 2000

00 01 02 03 04   1 2 3 4 5 6 7 8 9 10

Teddy Bear, Piglet, Kitten & Me

Words by Catherine Maccabe * Pictures by Clive Scruton

Augsburg Books
Bringing Families Together
for Children & Families

We went to the beach,
where the waves were so wild,

Much larger, dear God,
than one little child.

I know we are small,
but please, can you see
Teddy bear, piglet,
kitten, and me?

We went to the woods,
where the trees grow so high.

I can tell, if I look,
that they reach to the sky.

I know we are small,
but please, can you see
Teddy bear, piglet,
kitten, and me?

We went to the park,
where it started to rain.

There was thunder and lightning
and thunder again.

I know we are small,
but please, can you see
Teddy bear, piglet,
kitten, and me?

We went to the zoo,
where the elephants stay.

They're bigger than houses,
and too big to play.

I know we are small,
but please, can you see
Teddy bear, piglet,
kitten, and me?

We went to the town,
full of bustle and noise.

I nearly got lost
in the store that sells toys.

I know we are small,
but please, can you see

Teddy bear, piglet, kitten, and me?

We went to the church,
we walked through the snow.
Inside it was warm
in the candlelit glow.

I know we are small,
but I think you can see
Teddy bear, piglet,
kitten, and me?

We've come to the stable,
we followed the star.
Baby Jesus lies smiling,
we know who you are—

God's Son, oh, so small,
so of course you can see
Teddy bear, piglet,
kitten, and me.